FREEDOM
FOR ALL

The Inspiring True Story of the Statue of Liberty

Janet Palazzo-Craig

Troll

Freedom's Symbol: The Statue of Liberty

She stands proudly in New York harbor, welcoming all who come to the United States. Her face is strong and determined. Her right hand, reaching high into the sky, holds a bright torch. Its golden flame is the beacon of freedom. At her feet lies a broken chain, which symbolizes the defeat of those who would try to take away America's liberty. In her left hand she holds a tablet on which the date July 4, 1776, is written in Roman numerals. This is the date when the American colonies declared their independence from Great Britain and the Revolutionary War began. The giant structure wears a pointed crown upon her head. Its seven spikes are said to represent the light of freedom shining out around the world.

Who is this towering figure? She is the Statue of Liberty, a world-famous symbol of America and freedom. The pale green monument has stood on tiny Liberty Island for more than one hundred years. She has welcomed countless immigrants to America's shores. These people, who came from many countries, hoped to begin new lives in a land that would celebrate their special talents and cultures. Today, more than five million tourists visit Liberty Island every year to tour the famous statue. What is the history of the Statue of Liberty? How did she come to stand on a small island in Upper New York Bay? The story of the statue's creation is a fascinating true tale.

Liberty, a symbol of freedom, stands proudly in New York harbor.

A Monument to Freedom and Friendship

Did you know that the Statue of Liberty was a gift to the people of the United States from the people of France? In 1865, a French writer and historian named Édouard de Laboulaye proposed the idea of the statue. He was speaking to guests who were attending a dinner party in his home. He explained that the statue would be a present for America from the people of France. If it could be completed by 1876, the centennial of the American Revolution, the gift would celebrate one hundred years of freedom in the United States. The French had helped the Americans to gain their independence from Great Britain during the Revolutionary War. Laboulaye wanted the statue to stand forever as a symbol of freedom, and to be a token of the long friendship between America and France.

One of the guests at Laboulaye's dinner party was a handsome young man named Frédéric Auguste Bartholdi. He was a well-known sculptor who had already created many fine works of art. Laboulaye asked Bartholdi to make a giant statue for America. Bartholdi was happy to agree to Laboulaye's proposal. He liked the idea of designing grand public monuments, and he was intrigued by the project.

Bartholdi was asked to travel to the United States. He would meet with public officials to find out if America would accept such a gift. Bartholdi also planned to ask the Americans if they would be able to supply a proper pedestal, or base, for the statue to stand upon, as well as the land needed to exhibit the work.

Frédéric Auguste Bartholdi sculpted Liberty Enlightening the World,
known today as the Statue of Liberty.

Bartholdi did not go to America until 1871. He sailed for New York harbor on the French steamer *Pereire*. Many immigrants crossed the Atlantic Ocean with him.

After thirteen days at sea, the steamship entered the busy harbor. The immigrants, as well as Bartholdi, flocked to the deck of the *Pereire* to see their first glimpse of America. Bartholdi spotted a tiny island in Upper New York Bay, which was known as Bedloe's Island at the time. He decided Bedloe's Island would be the perfect home for his statue. He quickly sketched a rough watercolor painting of his idea. The sculptor imagined Liberty, with her flame of freedom held high above the open sea, welcoming immigrants to the New World.

Bartholdi stayed in America for five months. He met with many important people, including President Ulysses S. Grant. Grant approved of the project and of the proposed site. Bartholdi could not have been more delighted. The Americans wanted his statue!

Immigrants such as these traveled in great numbers to America during the late 1890s and early 1900s, arriving in New York harbor.

The Statue Takes Shape

When Bartholdi returned to France, he was ready to build the largest statue in the world. Laboulaye and his friends formed a committee called the French-American Union. They immediately began seeking donations from the French people to raise the money needed to build the monument.

Bartholdi, meanwhile, worked on a clay model of the statue. We know of at least two other sculptures that influenced his design. One was a huge bronze statue called the Colossus of Rhodes. This statue was built in the third century B.C., and it had been one of the Seven Wonders of the World. Although it was destroyed during an earthquake, descriptions of the giant sculpture say that it stood at the entrance to a harbor and held one arm aloft.

Bartholdi's design for the statue was also influenced by a project he had hoped to build in Egypt near the Suez Canal. He had wanted to sculpt a giant peasant woman holding a light. The statue was to serve as a lighthouse, but it was never built. Bartholdi used some of his ideas for this monument when creating the Statue of Liberty.

It is believed that Bartholdi modeled the statue's face after his mother. The figure's body and arms were inspired by a beautiful young woman Bartholdi knew named Jeanne-Emilie Bheux de Pusieux. Bartholdi and Jeanne-Emilie later married.

Charlotte Bartholdi, the sculptor's mother, is said to have been the model for Liberty's face.

Bartholdi experimented with many different concepts of Liberty, as shown by these small clay sculptures.

In 1875, Bartholdi finished the 4-foot-high clay model that would be used as the first step in the creation of the largest statue ever built. He called the figure *Liberty Enlightening the World*. Eventually, the monument became known as the Statue of Liberty.

The clay model was unveiled at a fund-raising dinner given by the French-American Union. Soon the committee had raised enough money for Bartholdi to begin building.

The creation of the enormous statue was a complex job. Bartholdi needed lots of space, so he rented a high-ceilinged studio in Paris. It is reported that at least twenty craftsmen worked ten hours a day for weeks at a time to complete certain parts of the statue. Bartholdi planned to build the final 151-foot-tall figure in sections. All the parts would be shipped to the United States and then pieced together like a puzzle. An engineer named Eugène Viollet-le-Duc suggested using copper for the huge, hollow structure because copper is a fairly light metal that can be shaped easily. Copper was also cheaper than bronze.

Before that could happen, however, Bartholdi needed to make several more models of the statue. Each model would be larger than the one before it. The first enlarged model was slightly more than twice the size of the original, or about $9\frac{1}{2}$ feet tall. The second enlarged model was four times bigger than the one before it, or about 38 feet high. This model was one quarter of the size that the finished statue would be, so it was called the *quarter-size model*. Bartholdi carefully studied this model because it would be his last chance to make changes before he began work on the finished sculpture.

At least twenty craftsmen worked long hours in Bartholdi's Paris studio to complete the Statue of Liberty.

Building the Full-Sized Statue

The final statue was built in segments. Bartholdi enlarged each section of his quarter-size model by four times to create the full-sized figure.

First, craftsmen built full-sized wooden sculptures of each section. Workers then covered the wooden shapes with plaster. Next, sculptors copied all the details from the quarter-size model onto the plaster. After that, carpenters built wooden forms that followed each line, curve, and fold around the outside of the plaster model. When the wooden forms were removed, the shape on the inside of each wooden form was the exact reverse of the plaster shape. For example, where the plaster model curved out, the wooden form curved in.

Metalworkers pushed thin sheets of copper into the wooden forms. The copper was only $^{3}/_{32}$ inch thick, which is about the thickness of two pennies placed one on top of the other. When the soft copper was hammered against the wooden form, a segment of the statue's final copper "skin" was created. The copper segment was pulled away from its wooden form, and it exactly matched the corresponding segment of the full-sized plaster model. This method of sculpting is called *repoussé*, a French word meaning "pushed back." It was Viollet-le-Duc's idea to use *repoussé*. The copper segment was now ready to be attached to the framework of the statue and *riveted*, or bolted, to other segments.

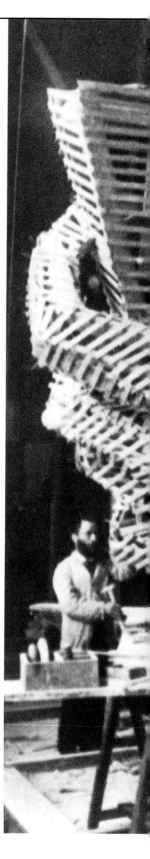

The full-sized wooden model of Liberty's hand is seen before the plaster was applied.

Although Bartholdi had hoped to have the entire statue ready by July 4, 1876, delays made that impossible. Instead, he and his staff worked hard to complete the statue's right hand and torch. They succeeded, and the enormous hand and flame were shipped to the Philadelphia Exposition in time for America's centennial celebration. At that time, the statue's copper skin was new, and it looked like a bright penny. Americans marveled at the huge segment of the statue. Hundreds of visitors climbed up to the viewing platform on the torch and looked out over the Exposition fairgrounds.

In 1876, Liberty's right hand and torch were shipped to the Philadelphia Exposition, where the colossal fragment was met with great enthusiasm.

Liberty's Skeleton: Eiffel's Wonderful Idea!

It is strange to think that Bartholdi began building his statue without really knowing how it would stand up. He realized that the heavy, hollow structure would need a "skeleton" of some kind to support the copper skin. The statue would also need to be able to withstand high winds and other weather conditions. But Bartholdi was a sculptor, not an engineer. He didn't know how to solve these problems.

The French engineer Gustave Eiffel designed the ingenious framework to hold up the giant statue.

A French engineer named Gustave Eiffel was asked to design a support system for the towering 32-ton statue. Eiffel was nicknamed the "magician of iron." He would achieve worldwide fame in 1889 for his best-known creation, the Eiffel Tower in Paris.

Eiffel's framework for the Statue of Liberty was anchored by a central support made of four iron columns. Crosspieces connected the four vertical columns. Thinner iron beams were then joined to the central support. Many short iron bars were attached to these beams. The short bars would be fastened to the inside of the statue's copper skin. In that way, the weight of each segment of the statue would rest on the central support columns, not on the segment below it.

A worker is shown inside the statue among the iron bars that were attached to the ribs running around the inside of the statue's skin.

The skin was not bolted directly to the short iron bars. Instead, Eiffel created iron "ribs" that ran along the inside of the statue. These ribs were then passed through curved copper "saddles," which were connected to the framework. This allowed the statue to move slightly in high winds and to expand and contract as the temperature changed. This flexibility made the statue stronger.

Inside the statue, Eiffel designed two parallel spiral staircases. Visitors could climb up to the crown on one staircase, then come back down on the other.

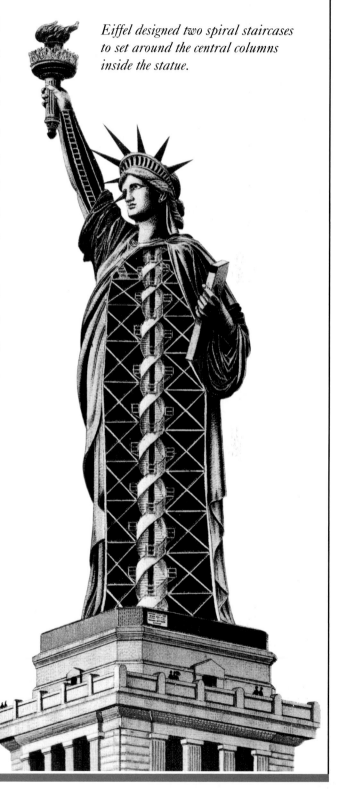

Eiffel designed two spiral staircases to set around the central columns inside the statue.

This view of the inside of the statue's enormous face shows how Eiffel's framework was designed.

America Faces a Problem: A Pedestal for Liberty

The statue was officially given to the citizens of the United States in a special ceremony in Paris on July 4, 1884. Before the monument could be assembled in America, however, a proper pedestal needed to be built.

Bedloe's Island became the statue's official site, as Bartholdi had hoped. (In 1956, Bedloe's Island was renamed Liberty Island.) There was an old star-shaped fort, called Fort Wood, on the island. This large building would serve as part of the foundation for the pedestal. Richard Morris Hunt, an American architect, designed a high concrete-and-granite pedestal, which would sit atop the fort. The pedestal and its foundation together would be 154 feet tall.

Richard Morris Hunt designed the massive pedestal upon which Liberty stands.

The American Committee for the Statue of Liberty was created to collect donations from Americans to build the pedestal. Meanwhile, the French were preparing to ship the statue to the United States. Where would Liberty stand if the pedestal was not built?

A man named Joseph Pulitzer decided to help. Pulitzer had arrived in America as a penniless immigrant from Hungary years earlier. He had become a wealthy newspaper owner. Pulitzer wrote in his paper that he would publish the name of each person who gave money to help build the pedestal, no matter how large or small the amount. His campaign was a success. Poor workers and schoolchildren, as well as wealthy Americans, donated $102,000 in five months.

The giant head and shoulders of Liberty were displayed in Paris during the campaign to raise funds for the project.

Home, at Last! The Statue's Dedication

Finally, the massive pedestal was built. The statue segments were unpacked from their crates, and the great project of assembling Liberty in her new home began.

On October 28, 1886, the statue was complete, and a huge celebration was planned for the monument's dedication. It was a rainy day, but the weather did not dampen the spirits of the many spectators who came to watch the unveiling.

Bartholdi, perched high in the statue's crown, held the ropes to the large French flag that covered Liberty's face. It was his job to unveil the statue. As he did so, cheering filled the air. Blasts from cannons and the whistles of steamships made a deafening roar. United States President Grover Cleveland attended the ceremony. Unfortunately, Édouard de Laboulaye, the man whose idea the statue had been, was not there. He had died in 1883. The statue he had first proposed in 1865 had taken more than twenty years to grow from a dream to a reality.

At last, Liberty was installed in her new home amid a great celebration.

The Statue of Liberty became an inspiring sight to the unending waves of immigrants who passed by it on their journey to Ellis Island during the late 1800s and early 1900s. The poet Emma Lazarus called the great statue the "Mother of Exiles." These words from her famous poem,

Emma Lazarus is the author of "The New Colossus," a poem that describes Liberty greeting the great waves of immigrants who passed through New York harbor.

entitled "The New Colossus," describe the statue as a symbol of the freedom from oppression that many immigrants still seek today:

Give me your tired, your poor,
Your huddled masses yearning to breathe free,
The wretched refuse of your teeming shore.
Send these, the homeless, tempest-tost, to me,
I lift my lamp beside the golden door!

Liberty Gets Help: A Giant Restoration Project

By the early 1980s, it was easy to see that Liberty was in need of repairs. Sections of the statue's copper skin had begun to rust. The torch leaked badly. Inside the statue, the iron ribs were badly rusted. Layers of grime, paint, and graffiti covered the walls. Liberty's head had also begun to lean.

It was decided that these things needed to be fixed before 1986, the hundredth anniversary of the statue's dedication. So in the early 1980s, a group called the French-American Committee for the Restoration of the Statue of Liberty was formed. This committee worked along with the National Park Service, which manages the statue, to fix the monument. They raised millions of dollars in donations to pay for the renovation.

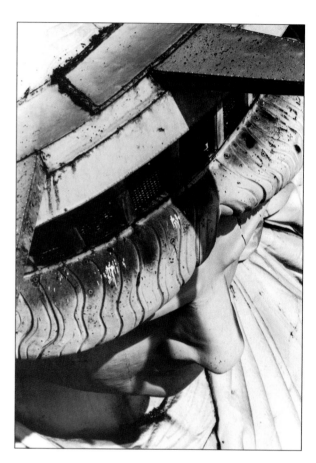

Liberty's nose was pitted and her crown leaked badly before the restoration.

In order to repair the outside of the statue, an enormous scaffold had to be built. It was separated from the statue's copper skin by 18 inches all around so that it would not damage the monument.

This gigantic scaffold was built all around the statue so repairs could take place.

During the repairs, the old flame was removed. A new one, modeled after Bartholdi's original plans, was constructed. Today the old torch is displayed near the statue's base, giving visitors a close look at a big piece of history.

Rusted iron ribs were replaced with new ones made from stainless steel. The outside of the statue was cleaned, but the famous green color of the copper was kept. The rusted iron framework was replaced, as were missing or rusted rivets.

New, separate up and down staircases were built inside the statue. A new elevator was installed in the base, an emergency elevator was added, and a new viewing platform was built at the crown.

At last, Liberty was ready for her birthday!

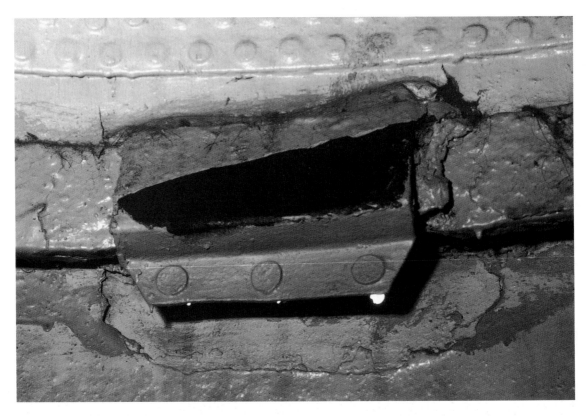

All the rusted and broken parts of the statue were replaced during its restoration.

Liberty's Centennial Celebration

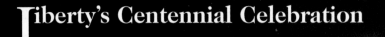

On July 3, 1986, an enormous party marking the Statue of Liberty's one hundredth birthday began. Eleven million people came to New York City to enjoy the celebrations, which included the relighting of the golden torch and the reopening of the statue to the public. Later, on October 28, 1986, President Ronald Reagan rededicated the statue. The date marked one hundred years exactly since the original dedication.

The statue seen at sunset as she lifts her beacon of freedom.

Freedom for All!

The Statue of Liberty is an inspiring sight, and the story of its creation is an important part of America's history. This beautiful monument, which was originally a gift of friendship, has become a beacon of freedom to people all over the world. This powerful symbol is a national treasure that deserves great care by those who revere it—the people of the United States and people everywhere who love freedom, justice, and friendship.

The Statue of Liberty has welcomed countless immigrants to Ellis Island and the promise of freedom.

Amazing Facts

Height of statue from feet to torch is 151 feet, 1 inch.

Height of foundation is 65 feet.

Height of pedestal is 89 feet.

Total height of monument is 305 feet, 1 inch.

Thickness of copper ranges from ⅛ inch to 3/32 inch.

Weight of copper skin is 32 tons.

Number of pedestal steps is 189.

Number of statue steps is 142.

Size of fingernail is 13 inches x 10 inches.

Eye is 2 feet, 6 inches wide.

Nose is 4 feet, 6 inches long.

Index finger is 8 feet long.

Mouth is 3 feet wide.

Right arm is 42 feet long.

Bibliography

Curlee, Lynn. *Liberty*. New York: Simon & Schuster, 2000.

encarta.msn.com, s.v. "Statue of Liberty."

Handlin, Oscar. *Statue of Liberty*. New York: Newsweek Books, 1971.

Hargrove, Jim. *Gateway to Freedom: The Story of the Statue of Liberty and Ellis Island*. Chicago: Children's Press, 1986.

Harris, Jonathan. *A Statue for America*. New York: Macmillan, 1985.

Krake, Robert. *The Statue of Liberty Comes to America*. Champaign, IL: Garrard, 1972.

Moreno, Barry: *The Statue of Liberty Encyclopedia*. New York: Simon & Schuster, 2000.

Shapiro, Mary J. *How They Built the Statue of Liberty*. New York: Random House, 1985.

_____. *Gateway to Liberty*. New York: Vintage Books, 1986.

Trachtenberg, Marvin. *The Statue of Liberty*. New York: Viking, 1976.

World Book Encyclopedia, 1999 ed., s.v. "Statue of Liberty."

www.americanparknetwork.com

Special thanks to Barry Moreno and Jeffrey Dosik at
the Statue of Liberty/Ellis Island Research Library for
their assistance.

Photographs are reprinted by courtesy of the Statue of
Liberty National Monument.

Text copyright © 2002 by Troll Communications L.L.C.

Published by Troll Communications L.L.C.

Designed by Shi Chen.

Printed in the United States of America.

10 9 8 7 6 5 4 3 2 1